Through
the Kitchen Window

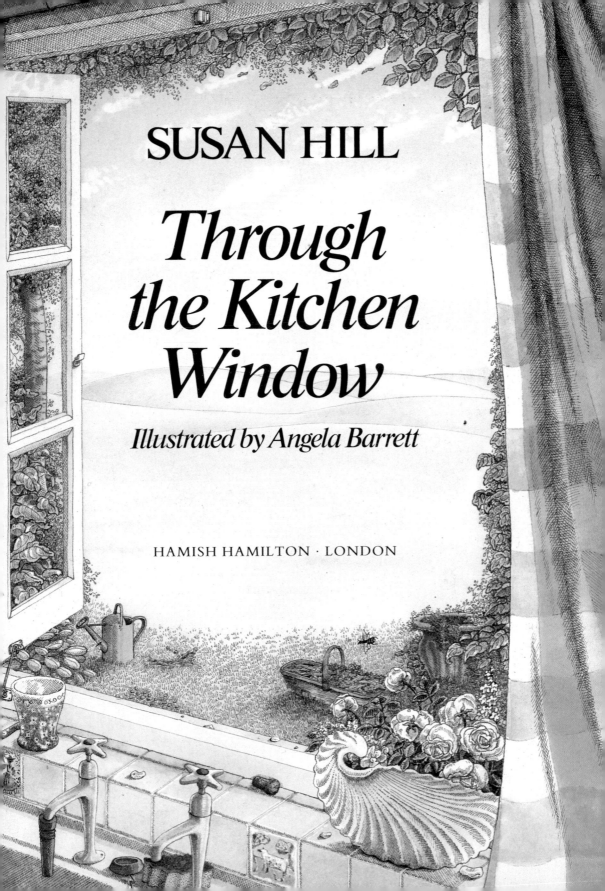

SUSAN HILL

Through the Kitchen Window

Illustrated by Angela Barrett

HAMISH HAMILTON · LONDON

First published in Great Britain 1984
by Hamish Hamilton Ltd
Garden House 57–59 Long Acre London WC2E 9JZ

Text copyright © 1984 by Susan Hill
Illustrations copyright © 1984 by Angela Barrett

British Library Cataloguing in Publication Data

Hill, Susan, 1942–
Through the kitchen window.
1. Home economics—Handbooks, manuals, etc.
I. Title
640   TX159
ISBN 0-241-11350-4

Filmset by Servis Filmsetting Ltd, Manchester
Printed and bound in Italy by Arnoldo Mondadori Editore, Verona

Winter

The Winter Kitchen

IN WINTER, the kitchen is the heart of the house. It is a living place. Kettles sing, pots simmer, pans bubble. Visitors come to sit in the kitchen, children use the kitchen table, to draw at, paint at, model plasticine upon. And to help with the cooking. They hang about, waiting for bowls to lick out.

There is a chair for quiet reading, and waiting for this or that to be put in or taken out of the oven, to be ready, to be kneaded or turned or basted or stirred.

Beside the stove, cats purr with half-closed eyes.

In winter, the kitchen is always warm, and, always, there are smells: of roasting meat and stewing soups, frying onions and baking bread. There is the chop-chop-chop of the knife, through carrots and turnips and mounds of fresh leeks, and the rhythmic pulse of the electric beater. And, in the sudden silence after it has stopped, the ticking of the clock.

In winter, the kitchen windows are steamed over, and pin-men and names and smiling sunny faces are drawn across the panes with chubby fingers.

Outside, early dark, rain like a whip lash, gale and hail, rattling the latch, or ice, sealing it tight.

But inside, all is bright, warm, savoury, companionable.

Winter Tea

IT is mid-winter, dark December. It is Sunday afternoon. In boots and greatcoats, mufflers and mittens, everyone has gone for a walk, except perhaps for grandmama and great-aunt, who snooze beside the fire, and the cats, stretched sleek on the hearthrug.

They have gone across the fields towards the wood. The air is damp, raw, cold, it catches the breath. Early this morning, and late tonight, comes the frost, hardening the earth.

The men are carrying guns, and slung about with rabbits and pigeons. The children are tumbling and gambolling and racing in zig-zags, voices carrying on the still, chill air. Stamping of feet, blowing on fingers, beating of arms.

And now the sun sets, rose-red and blazing, below the hill.

Bones ache, teeth chatter, skin chaps, noses run. They are heading for home, and, in the house ahead, the lamps come on in welcome, and the clock stirs, gathers itself, then chimes.

It is time for tea.

The table, laid for high tea in winter, is a rich delight. There are the plates and bowls and dishes piled high with good things, and the singing kettle and the great teapot-stand at the centre of all.

This is not a genteel meal, and never at all formal; there is no dressing-up, for high tea. It is a convivial comfort, satisfying, noisy. It is a knife-and-fork, a meat tea, a proper meal.

There are cold hams and round tongues and pressed beef, all pink, to be sliced thickly, and with them goes strong, bright mustard and horse-radish that brings tears to the eyes, and glass jars of pickles, dipped into with a silver fork, onions, small, crunchy and vinegar-sour, yellow piccallilli and dark, brown, thick, sweet chutney. Red cabbage, tiny, burgundy beets.

There are salads, not the limp lettuce and bland tomatoes out-of-season, but winter salads with a bite to them, of shredded cabbage and hearty chicory, pungent celery and sharp apple dotted about with raisin.

And with the meats, or after them, come the savoury pies. A raised pork pie like an upturned hat, oozing its jelly. A cold bacon and egg pie, solid and substantial with pastry top and bottom. A sausagemeat and onion

plate pie, a veal and ham, and scotch eggs in their crumbly coats, and little, flakey sausage rolls that dissolve in the mouth.

After the meats, the sweets: the trifle in its cut glass bowl, layered red and buttery yellow and cream, fancifully set about with blobs and whorls, and here a cherry, there a strip of green angelica.

Loaves. White and brown, for spreading with butter and jam. Tea-loaves, sticky-topped malt, packed with fruit, bara brith and currant loaf, date and walnut and lardy cake and honey and apple, all brown, all moist.

Cakes. Round cakes, plain and heavy, or airy sponges, dusted with sugar, scattered with nuts, inch-deep in fondant icing. A seed cake, a dark, dark Dundee, its surface stuck around and around with toasted almonds. Victoria Sandwich, light as air, Devil's food, wickedly rich. A lemon cake, warm, pricked all over with a skewer and the holes filled with fresh lemon syrup that soaks in and runs over on to the plate.

Plates are piled with biscuits, ginger and flapjack and shortbread and Shrewsbury.

Under covers, hot muffins, crumpets, griddle scones, and cinnamon toast, golden with butter.

High tea in winter is a meal-for-the-day, and for the cold and the dark, a meal for all ages, appetites and fancies. A meal like no other.

Sausage and Onion Plate Pie
8 oz shortcrust pastry (savoury)
8 oz pork sausage meat
1 large onion
1 large egg
Mixed thyme, marjoram and sage, dried

Choose a 7–8-inch pie plate. Line with pastry.

Mix together the meat, chopped onion, beaten egg and herbs, thoroughly. Season with pepper. Fill the pie and cover with a pastry lid. Prick a couple of holes with a fork.

Bake for half an hour in a hot oven.

Fruity Tea Bread
6 oz mixed dried fruit
1 oz chopped, mixed peel
Tea cup of cold tea, strained
4 oz clear honey
1 egg
8 oz self-raising flour
1 oz melted butter
Pinch salt

Soak the fruit, peel and honey in the tea overnight in a bowl.

Next day, stir in beaten egg, then sifted flour and salt, then butter.

Bake in a 1-lb loaf-tin for forty-five minutes. Remove. Brush with more melted honey, and scatter with a few chopped walnuts and demerara sugar. Return to the oven for a further thirty minutes. (Moderate oven, 180 C, gas mark 4.)

Lemon Cake
4 oz melted butter
4 oz caster sugar
1 egg
1 lemon
4 oz self-raising flour

Mix melted butter with 2 oz of the sugar and beaten egg. Grate lemon rind finely and fold into this mixture, then add the flour.

Grease a 7-inch sandwich tin, put in cake mixture and bake for twenty minutes in a moderate oven.

Turn out on to a plate, an while warm quickly make a few pricks with a fork or skewer and spoon over the juice of the lemon, mixed with the remaining 2 oz of sugar.

Serve warm.

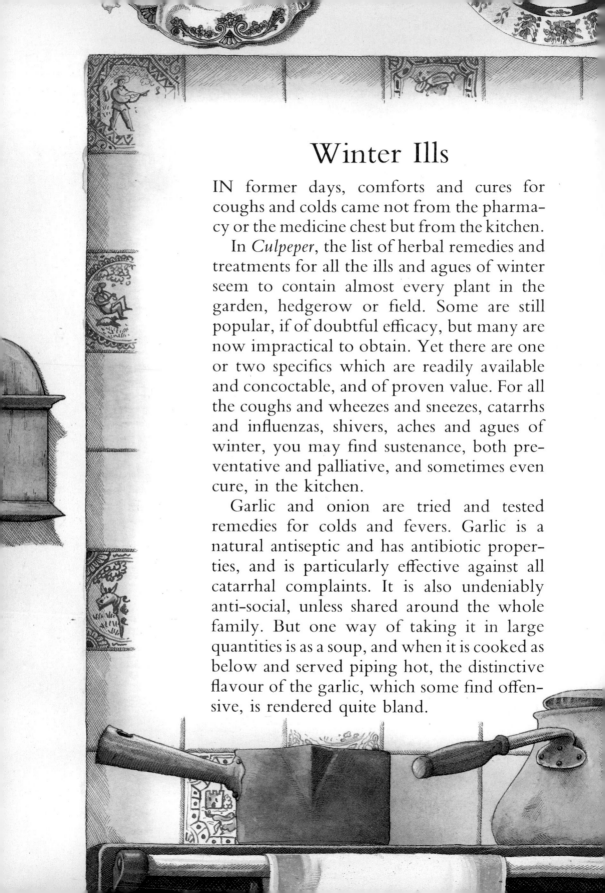

Winter Ills

IN former days, comforts and cures for coughs and colds came not from the pharmacy or the medicine chest but from the kitchen.

In *Culpeper*, the list of herbal remedies and treatments for all the ills and agues of winter seem to contain almost every plant in the garden, hedgerow or field. Some are still popular, if of doubtful efficacy, but many are now impractical to obtain. Yet there are one or two specifics which are readily available and concoctable, and of proven value. For all the coughs and wheezes and sneezes, catarrhs and influenzas, shivers, aches and agues of winter, you may find sustenance, both preventative and palliative, and sometimes even cure, in the kitchen.

Garlic and onion are tried and tested remedies for colds and fevers. Garlic is a natural antiseptic and has antibiotic properties, and is particularly effective against all catarrhal complaints. It is also undeniably anti-social, unless shared around the whole family. But one way of taking it in large quantities is as a soup, and when it is cooked as below and served piping hot, the distinctive flavour of the garlic, which some find offensive, is rendered quite bland.

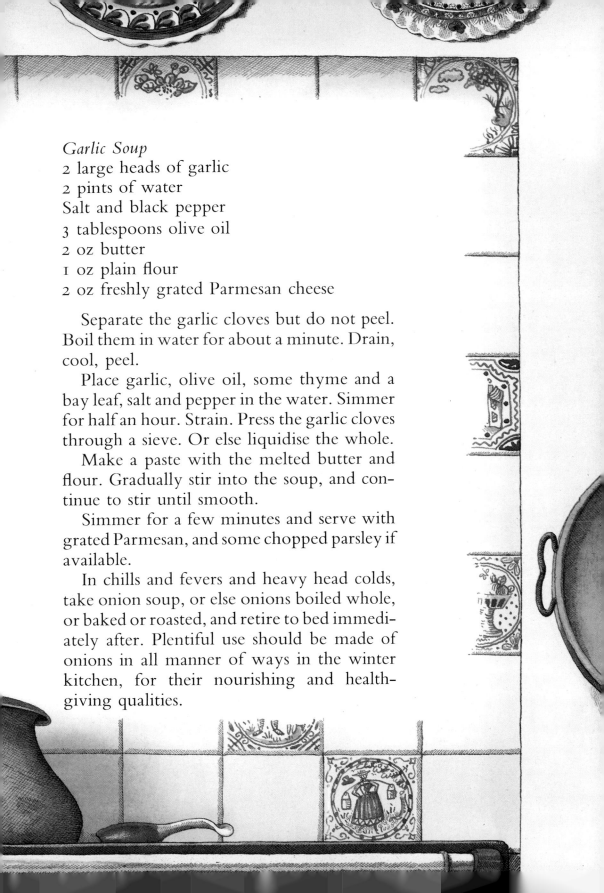

Garlic Soup
2 large heads of garlic
2 pints of water
Salt and black pepper
3 tablespoons olive oil
2 oz butter
1 oz plain flour
2 oz freshly grated Parmesan cheese

Separate the garlic cloves but do not peel. Boil them in water for about a minute. Drain, cool, peel.

Place garlic, olive oil, some thyme and a bay leaf, salt and pepper in the water. Simmer for half an hour. Strain. Press the garlic cloves through a sieve. Or else liquidise the whole.

Make a paste with the melted butter and flour. Gradually stir into the soup, and continue to stir until smooth.

Simmer for a few minutes and serve with grated Parmesan, and some chopped parsley if available.

In chills and fevers and heavy head colds, take onion soup, or else onions boiled whole, or baked or roasted, and retire to bed immediately after. Plentiful use should be made of onions in all manner of ways in the winter kitchen, for their nourishing and health-giving qualities.

Fruits and fresh fruit juices are vital to strengthen the natural resistance to the ills of winter, as well as for those who have already succumbed.

Citrus fruits are imported in great quantities and at their freshest, juiciest and best between November and February, so that lemons and oranges for squeezing or pressing are easily and cheaply obtainable, and fill the kitchen with a wonderful, sharp scent of hot Mediterranean and tropical places.

A hot toddy is a pleasure in any state of cold or chill. Fresh lemon juice is mixed with boiling water, sweetened with honey, and given a generous dash of whisky or rum or brandy.

But a patient with a fever does not want to be further overheated, and then, copious cool drinks are required, to replace body fluids and ease sore throats and dry mouths.

Auntie Pam's Lemon Drink
2 or 3 lemons, thinly peeled. Rind and juice
1 lb sugar
1 oz citric acid
1 pint boiling water

Put lemons, sugar and citric acid into a large jug. Pour on the boiling water, and stir until sugar dissolves.
Cover. Leave to cool, stirring occasionally.
Dilute to taste.
Keeps about ten days in a refrigerator.

Christmas

CHRISTMAS in the kitchen begins in October. Then, the cake, the mincemeat and the pudding are made, and then, the smells of Christmas cooking begin to seep through the house, to linger there, in cracks and corners, until December.

It is spicy, hinting of exotic places. There is cinnamon from Sri Lanka, there are cloves from Zanzibar, there is ginger from China and Jamaica, nutmeg from the tree called *Myrtica fragrans* that grows in the Indies.

On the table, bowls of dried fruit in dark, glistening mounds, currants, raisins, sultanas, dates, with piles of chopped peel and strips of crystallised citrus, and cherries stickily soaked in sugar. Crumbly creamy suet, pith and zest of oranges and lemons, together with apples, Blenheims and Bramleys, Lambourne and Cox, all neatly chopped.

Everyone comes in to stir the pudding and the fumes of the brandy rise up. The wishes are all made. Christmas has begun.

A Christmas Dinner

"Such a bustle ensued that you might have thought a goose the rarest of all birds; a feathered phenomenon, to which a black swan was a matter of course – and in truth, it was something very like it in that house. Mrs Cratchit made the gravy (ready beforehand in a little saucepan) hissing hot; Master Peter mashed the potatoes with incredible vigour;

Miss Belinda sweetened up the apple sauce; Martha dusted the hot plates; Bob took Tiny Tim beside him in a tiny corner of the table; the two young Cratchits set chairs for everybody, not forgetting themselves, and mounting guard upon their posts, crammed spoons into their mouths, lest they should shriek for goose before their turn came to be helped. At last the dishes were set on, and grace was said. It was succeeded by a breathless pause, as Mrs Cratchit, looking slowly all along the carving-knife, prepared to plunge it in the breast; but when she did, and when the long expected gush of stuffing issued forth, one murmur of

delight arose all around the board, and even Tiny Tim, excited by the two young Cratchits, beat on the table with the handle of his knife, and feebly cried, Hurrah!

"There never was such a goose. Bob said he didn't believe there ever was such a goose cooked. Its tenderness and flavour, size and cheapness, were the themes of universal admiration. Eked out by the apple sauce and mashed potatoes, it was a sufficient dinner for the whole family; indeed, as Mrs Cratchit said with great delight (surveying one small atom of a bone upon the dish) they hadn't ate it all at last! Yet every one had had enough and the youngest Cratchits in particular were steeped in sage and onion to the eyebrows! But now, the plates being changed by Miss Belinda, Mrs Cratchit left the room alone – too nervous to bear witnesses – to take the pudding up and bring it in.

"Suppose it should not be done enough! Suppose it should break on turning out! Suppose somebody should have got over the wall of the backyard, and stolen it, while they were merry with the goose – a supposition at which the two young Cratchits became livid! All sorts of horrors were supposed.

"Hallo! A great deal of steam! The pudding was out of the copper. A smell like a washing day! That was the cloth. A smell like an eating-house and a pastrycook's next door to each other, with a laundress's next door to that! That was the pudding! In half a minute,

Mrs Cratchit entered – flushed but smiling proudly – with the pudding like a speckled cannonball so hard and firm and blazing in half of half-a-quartern of lighted brandy, and bedight with Christmas holly stuck into the top.

"Oh, a wonderful pudding! Bob Cratchit said, and calmly too, that he regarded it as the greatest success achieved by Mrs Cratchit since their marriage."

Charles Dickens: *A Christmas Carol*

Winter Puddings

Winter days are for proper puddings, rib-sticking, suety, satisfying puddings, thick, sustaining and sweet.

Marmalade pudding and treacle pudding, steamed or boiled.

Jam sponge, and spiced fruit from a white cloth.

And the puddings with the pretty names.
Guard's Pudding.
Castle Pudding.
Cabinet Pudding.
Poor Knights of Windsor.
Queen of Puddings.
Parson's Pudding.
Sussex Pond Pudding.
College Pudding.
Quaking Pudding.
Roly Poly.
Spotted Dick.

Marmalade

There is one certain way to cheer yourself up, on January days, when Christmas is quite over, and the spring still far ahead, when outside it is grey and cold, windy or wet or snow-bound – make marmalade.

The smells of marmalade-making are the best of winter: boiling sugar, tangy-sharp juices squirting up as you peel and grate, and your hands growing orangey-oily and aromatic. And the colours of the fruit, sevilles, lemons, grapefruit, all tumbled together, bring the sunshine of hot, exotic, far countries, into the house.

There are all manner of recipes for marmalade; with ginger and with grapefruit, or laced with brandy or whisky; honeyed, jellied, very dark, very pale, very thin, very

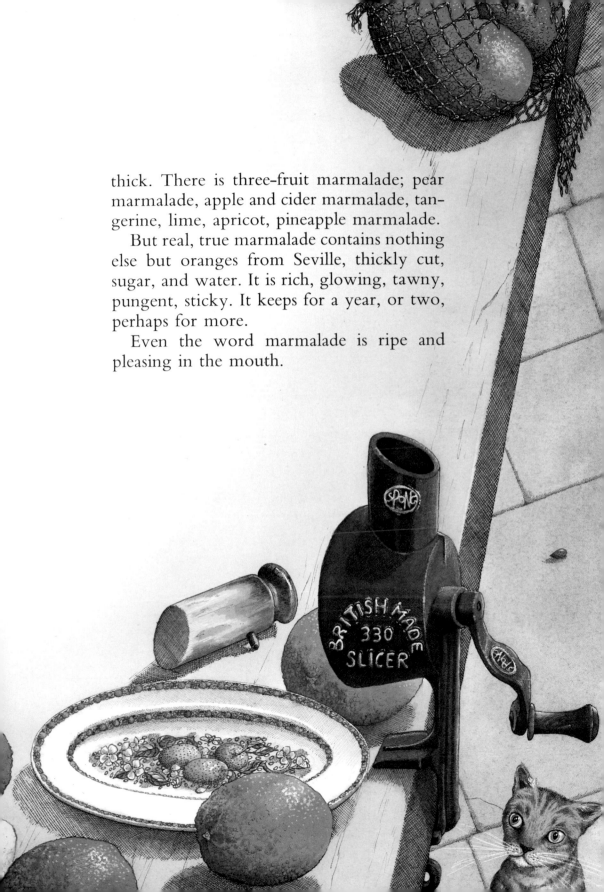

thick. There is three-fruit marmalade; pear marmalade, apple and cider marmalade, tangerine, lime, apricot, pineapple marmalade.

But real, true marmalade contains nothing else but oranges from Seville, thickly cut, sugar, and water. It is rich, glowing, tawny, pungent, sticky. It keeps for a year, or two, perhaps for more.

Even the word marmalade is ripe and pleasing in the mouth.

Ten Pleasures of the Winter Kitchen

THE bubble-bubble of soups and broths, the simmer of the stock-pot.

A dish of citrus fruits, jaffa and navel and blood oranges, tangerines and clementines, globular grapefruit, dozens of lemons, skins all aglow.

Root vegetables freshly pulled, earth still clinging to them and crumbling on to the table. Turnip and parsnip, carrot and celery, leek and swede.

A red cabbage, sliced down the centre, to reveal its whorls and whirls of purple-red-blue, inter-streaked with white.

A pomegranate, split open to reveal the same symmetry, perfectly satisfying to the eye.

A brace of pheasants hung up in the cool larder, tiny eyes red-rimmed, heads lolling, but feathers soft and strangely iridescent.

Blood in a dish from a hare or a haunch of venison.

The feel of the heavy Christmas pudding mixture as you stir, pulling on the hand and wrist and arm, resisting.

The rise and fall of the singing kettle as it boils for hot drinks on bitter days.

The dry smell of the shed where the onions and potatoes are stored, on strings or in sacks, and the other smell, of the apple loft under the eaves.

Spring

Spring Cleaning

ON THE first day of spring, whenever that may be, any day of March, April or May, the sky is swept clear of cloud and rain and winter murk, the morning sun shines in through the kitchen window, and there is a little warmth in it.

Start to spring clean, very early.

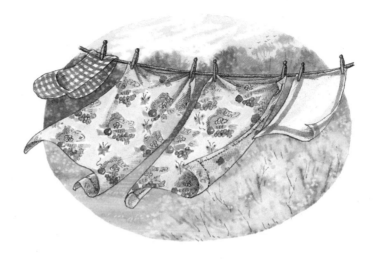

Turn out cupboards. Sweep to the back, clearing all the debris of spilled rice and sugar and currants and dead ants; rub away the sticky round rings of jam and marmalade. Throw out half-empty packets and half-full jars with lost lids, and dented cans and unlabelled bottles. Rip off the dirty shelf papers. Brush cobwebs from corners.

Soon, everything smells of hot soapy water, and woodwork drying slowly in the sun and the spring breeze blowing through the open door.

And then, if you can, whitewash walls, with a wide flat brush, slip-slap-slop in the pail.

And later, sit out on the step and turn your face up to the first spring sunshine and, like Mole, "Hang whitewash!"

Easter

EASTER weather is unpredictable, because the celebration may fall anywhere between late March and the end of April. But whether nor'easterly gales howl, clouds scud or snow flurries, or there is a balmy breeze and pale sunshine, whether the trees are still gaunt and winter-bare, or in the first flush of spring leaf, there are certain dishes which will always be eaten with pleasure.

Good Friday may no longer be a fast day, as ordained by the Church, but for many it remains a day for quiet reflection and self-restraint, and a plain supper based upon fresh fish is popular.

In Scandinavia, a traditional accompaniment to the Good Friday main course is Janssen's Temptation.

Janssen's Temptation
3 large onions
2 lb waxy potatoes
2 tins anchovies
$\frac{1}{2}$ pint single cream or cream mixed with top of the milk
3 oz butter

Peel and thinly slice the onions and cut the potatoes into strips like matchsticks.

Grease a shallow oven dish. Arrange a layer of potatoes, criss-cross with a lattice of anchovies, arrange the onions, finish with another layer of potatoes. Pour over half the cream, then the anchovy oil and dot with butter. Season with black pepper.

Bake in a very hot oven for an hour, until the potatoes are browning. Pour over the remaining cream. Cook a further thirty minutes.

For children's tea on Easter Saturday, there is a simple pudding which never fails to please, and serving it can become a family tradition.

Fried Eggs

Bake a plain sponge cake in a shallow tin. Turn it out, cool, place on a dish with room around the edge.

Place halved, tinned or poached fresh apricots on the sponge, hollows-down, leaving gaps between. Around each one, carefully pipe or spread whipped cream to look like the whites of eggs. Serve with orange jelly made of the apricot juices and water, around the base of the whole.

Easter Monday Treat

A pile of paper-thin pancakes, sprinkled with caster sugar and lemon juice, or with honey or treacle or maple syrup trickled over, or rolled up with mincemeat in the middle, or stuffed with apple puree into which crystallised ginger and raisins have been chopped. Or with a puree of raspberries and strawberries from the freezer.

Easter Biscuits
8 oz plain flour
Pinch salt
½ teaspoon cinnamon
4 oz butter
3 oz caster sugar
3 oz currants
1 beaten egg
A little milk
1 oz candied peel, chopped

Sift flour, salt and cinnamon. Rub in butter. Stir in sugar, currants and peel. Form into a stiff dough with the egg, and some milk if necessary. Chill the dough for at least one hour.

Roll out thinly. Cut into rounds.

Bake on a baking sheet, at 200 C, gas mark 6, until they are pale beige. (About fifteen–twenty minutes.) Cool on a tray. Brush with milk, sprinkle with sugar.

Magic

Bread baked on Good Friday will keep for seven years, and a loaf of it hung in the barn will keep rats and mice away.

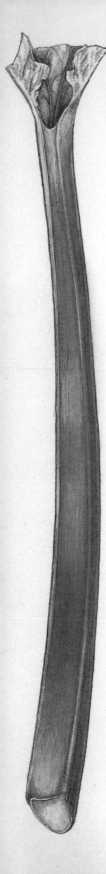

Rhubarb

AS early as February, thick sticks of the palest blush-pink forced rhubarb appear in the shops and, not long afterwards, begin to shoot up in the garden. It is the least troublesome of fruits to grow; it will settle very happily at the bottom of any patch, however scruffy, and though it appreciates a little attention, by way of fertiliser occasionally, it will survive the grossest neglect. Its great, umbrageous leaves are handsome, though deadly poisonous, and if allowed to run to seed it sends up tall, ferny heads of strange beauty.

But the fruit is coarse and unpleasant if left to thicken at the waist. Pull it young and tender; steam it and it will never disintegrate into a mush, but remain firm and shapely.

Rhubarb combines excellently with orange. Sprinkle with demerara sugar and squeeze the fresh juice over it. Or else with ginger: steep it in ginger syrup overnight.

It is dull and slimy as jam, schoolish with custard, but makes a light, frothy fool that melts in the mouth.

Rhubarb Fool

Young rhubarb, cut into thick chunks. Steam for five or ten minutes, until tender but still firm. While still warm, mix with juice of one orange, 2 oz vanilla sugar, 1 oz melted butter. Stand for fifteen minutes. Cool.

Make a custard with $\frac{1}{4}$ pint cream and 3 egg yolks in a double saucepan. Stir until thickened. Cool.

Mix with the puree. Pour into glasses. Top with whipped cream if liked. Decorate with slivers of orange peel and crystallised ginger. Serve with sponge fingers.

Asparagus

"SPEEDILY boiled, as not to lose the verdure and agreeable tenderness; which is done by letting the water boil before you put them in. I do not esteem the Dutch great and larger sort so sweet and agreeable as those of a moderate size."

John Evelyn

"The whole vegetable tribe have lost their zest for me. Only I stick to asparagus which still seems to inspire gentle thoughts."

Charles Lamb

Asparagus is best boiled or steamed, and served hot with melted butter or an hollandaise sauce. But strips of the thinnest sticks, sometimes called sprue, can be chopped and folded into an omelette or scrambled eggs.

To make elaborate soufflés and soups of asparagus, to roll it in damp bread or immobilise it in aspic, is simply to waste it.

Vanilla Sugar

FILL a glass jar with caster sugar. Insert a fresh vanilla pod. Put on an airtight lid. Keep for at least a week before using. A delicate flavour, quite different from that imparted by bitter, bottled vanilla essence.

Eggs

SPRING is for eggs. Fresh eggs, from hens allowed to roam and forage freely. Eggs, brown and white and speckled, smooth and satisfyingly shaped, heaped up in a bowl.

Eggs, whipped until frothy, eggs fried and looking like daisies, eggs with yolks with colour of buttercups.

Eggs, hard–boiled and painted with faces or ornamental patterns, eggs stained and dyed with vegetable juices and banded all the colours of the rainbow, and, later, rolled down grassy slopes.

Eggs Florentine. Eggs poached or soft-boiled, laid on a bed of cooked spinach, covered with a light cheese sauce and cooked until bubbling brown. If you feel fanciful, gather sorrel leaves or the tops of young nettles to puree instead of the spinach.

Never freeze eggs, or even store in a refrigerator. But they can be kept easily by rubbing each fresh egg over carefully between the hands with melted butter or dripping until every bit of shell is covered. Store in tins without lids but covered in greaseproof or brown paper tied with string.

Egg Sandwiches

Mash hardboiled eggs while still warm, with butter or a little cream, plenty of salt and pepper, some chopped tarragon or chervil. Chill slightly. Spread on crustless slices of wholemeal bread, topped with cress or water-cress if liked.

Eggs and Herbs

Tarragon is one of the most distinctive and versatile of herbs, and marries perfectly with eggs, and with chicken. Be sure you do not get Russian tarragon, which is bitter, but only French. Although it looks extremely delicate, tarragon will survive a harsh winter outdoors, in a sheltered spot, better than some of the tougher-looking herbs, such as rosemary.

Baked Eggs and Tarragon or Chervil

Scald single cream with plenty of chopped tarragon, or chervil. Leave to stand for half an hour, covered.

Break one egg per person into a buttered ramekin dish. Stand these in a roasting tin, with hot water to come half way up the sides.

Bake in a moderate oven until just set. Pour cream over each. Return to the oven for four minutes more. Sprinkle with more chopped herbs. Serve at once.

Elderflowers

GREAT foamy creamy white curds of blossom fill the lanes and hedgerows at the end of May, when spring takes a leap over the ditch into summer.

They have a most pungent and evocative scent and flavour, a little like that of the Muscatel grape.

Steep them in boiled water, leave to cool, strain. Use to rinse the face. An excellent skin tonic.

Add elderflowers to the first, sharp, small gooseberries, poached in syrup and made into a flan or pie. Or make a gooseberry and elderflower jam. Tie the flowers in a muslin bag, and suspend over the boiling jam mixture. Draw out before potting. The flavours marry perfectly.

Elderflowers make fine wine and champagne, fragrant and light. As a refreshing drink, diluted with spring water, try Elderflower Cordial.

Elderflower Cordial
25 elderflower heads
2 lb sugar
2 lemons, grated. squeezed, cut into small pieces
2 oz citric acid
2 pints cold, boiled water

Remove stems from flower heads and place in a large bowl. Add sugar, lemons, citric acid.

Cover with the water and leave for two days, stirring occasionally.

Strain. Bottle. Dilute to taste. Keep in a refrigerator.

Elderflower Water Ice
6 oz sugar
1 pint water
1 egg white
Juice of 2 and rind of 3 lemons
4–6 elderflower heads

Combine everything except egg white and lemon juice. Stir over a low heat until sugar dissolves. Boil for ten minutes.

Cool. Add lemon juice. Strain carefully.

Freeze about one hour, until slushy. Beat, with a fork or hand whisk. Stiffly beat the egg white, and fold it in. Freeze one further hour. Stir.

Then leave in freezer until needed. Thaw slightly before bringing to the table.

A Spring Dinner Menu

Fresh asparagus with butter

Poached fresh salmon

Roast leg of English spring lamb
with rosemary

New potatoes New carrots Spinach

A green salad, of lettuce, with small
raw spinach leaves, dandelion, sorrel
and nettle leaves, and watercress

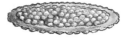

Gooseberry tart

Elderflower water ice
Mint water ice

Summer

IN SUMMER, the kitchen is not for lingering in, only for preparing food quickly, wrapping it or dishing it up, and taking it outside.

The stillroom and the larder and the dairy are dim and stone-slabbed and pleasingly cool. Jugs and bowls and dishes stand, muslin-covered. Cotton bags of whey drip, drip, drip

down, leaving the creamy yellow curds of cheese.

The refrigerator hums and vibrates day and night, a living creature in the corner. But the range stands cold and silent.

A pot of basil on the table, a pungent sweet geranium on the windowsill, a bunch of mint hung from the ceiling will all help to keep out summer flies.

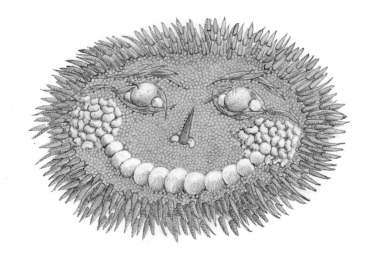

Vegetables

THE MARKET stalls are piled high with all the fresh vegetables of summer, but they are never better, never more tender, sweet and succulent than when picked young and straight from the garden just before cooking.

Then, a dish of vegetables is a feast all by itself. Tiny broad beans, the smallest of peas, the earliest, slenderest French beans, pale yellow carrots, creamy turnip-globes, no bigger than golf-balls with lilac-tinged tops, finger-sized courgettes, new potatoes like large marbles. These can be steamed all together, dressed in a very little butter, and every mouthful will taste of the earth and the summer season and of its own particular self.

Later in the summer, everything comes in abundance, thick and fast: you have a glut of whatever you grow.

Walk into the greenhouse, dark and shady during the day with the thick growth of tomato plants. Close your eyes and breathe in the heady, pungent, strange warm smell.

Summer Soups

Make in quantity, freeze in plastic bowls until needed, sprinkle with chopped green herbs, chives, parsley, mint.

Summer soups are green, made with cooked, pureed lettuce, or watercress or spinach or cucumber, blended with a little flour or potato, stirred into a light chicken stock, enriched with cream.

Midsummer Eve

On this enchanted night, witches and sprites and all manner of evil spirits are abroad. Sprigs of fennel or rowan brought into the house will afford protection.

Picnics

THERE is food for the hot August beach, eaten with salt-tasting, sand-encrusted fingers.

Food wrapped up well and carried in a knapsack, to devour, sitting high up on a hill, at the end of a long climb. Hearty food.

Home-made Scotch eggs, wrapped in spicy sausage-meat and dipped in crunchy, toasted brown breadcrumbs.

Hunks of cold pie and pasty.

Sausage and Apple Pasties

Rectangles of wholemeal pastry, filled with a mixture of sausage-meat, chopped onion and apple, seasoned, then folded, sealed, brushed with milk. Baked for forty-five minutes in a hot oven.

All manner of cold savoury flans, using cheese, onion, bacon, smoked fish, tomato.

Cold egg and bacon pie with a glazed crust.
Individual, raised pork pies, oozing jelly.
Sausage rolls in cheesy pastry.
Little cheese and anchovy tartlets.
Courgette flans. Spinach flans.
The best summer eating is out of doors.

There are blue skies with a puff or two of cloud, warm sunshine, the lightest of breezes.

Then, take a boat on the river. Glide gently downstream, hands dabbling through the weed-fronded water. Come to rest against the bank, under the shade of over-reaching willows. Spread a checked cloth upon the grass. Open the wicker basket with a creak.

Rat and Mole had just such a picnic.

There is the food to be eaten off delicately patterned bone china plates, at a table set down on the lawn under the spreading cedar tree. Dainty, genteel, afternoon-tea food.

Cucumber sandwiches, with white, crustless bread, both sliced paper-thin.

Creamy egg and cress sandwiches with brown bread.

Tiny strawberry tartlets, served with clotted cream or cream cheese hearts.

Coeur à la Crême
8 oz curd cheese
2 eggs
2 oz caster sugar
$\frac{1}{2}$ oz gelatine
8 oz double or whipping cream
6 tablespoons hot water

Sieve cheese until smooth, blend with egg yolks and sugar.

Dissolve gelatine in water. Cool. Whip into the cream, then fold lightly into cheese mixture.

Whip egg whites stiffly. Fold in.

Line china mould(s) with damp muslin or stockinette. Pour in cheese mixture. Fold the muslin over to cover. Refrigerate until set. Turn out.

★   ★   ★   ★

On rare, perfectly still evenings of high summer, there is food to be cooked outside, over charcoal. Plain cuts of best-quality meat, well marinaded in oil and wine vinegar, with some fresh herbs and seasoning, and grilled very hot and fast. Served with a tossed salad and garlic or herb bread.

Salads

A GOOD French dressing has a multitude of uses. Use best, cold-pressed olive or walnut oil, three parts, to one part of lemon juice and wine vinegar, with a pinch of dry mustard powder, salt, black pepper, and half a teaspoon caster sugar.

Tossed Green Salads

Lettuce, Cos, Webbs Wonderful, Butter-crunch, only the tender leaves.

Curly endive, young spinach leaves, water-cress, chopped celery, diced sharp apple.

Lovage, tarragon, chopped mint leaves.

Chopped shallots, crushed garlic, walnuts.

Cucumber salad. Wafer-thin slices, arranged on a flat dish, sprinkled with chopped fennel leaves. Dressed.

New potato salad. Waxy potatoes, dressed when still warm.

Brown rice. Cooked, cooled slightly, dressed, topped with chunks of cucumber or tuna fish.

Tomatoes. Sliced, covered with chopped fresh basil leaves, dressed.

A wicker basket of bread. Small, warm brown and white rolls. A plaited white loaf, sprinkled with poppy seeds.

Fruit

IN JUNE and July, the kitchen is full of bowls and baskets of fruit, heaps of strawberries and raspberries, gooseberries and loganberries and cherries, red- and white- and black-currants, glistening and richly-ripe.

They may be made into jams and jellies, pies and puddings, creams and fools, sauces and purees and cordials, or else bottled and frozen and crystallised or otherwise preserved for eating later in the year.

But best of all, eat them at once, whole and raw and fresh and in great quantities, greedily, steeped in sugar and thick, yellow cream.

Or in that fragrant, juice-seeping, parcel of perfection fruits, summer pudding.

Summer Pudding
Line a basin with slices of white, crustless bread, leaving no chinks between.

Take 1 lb raspberries, $\frac{1}{2}$ lb red currants, $\frac{1}{4}$ lb black-currants. Rinse and prepare carefully. Cook with 4 oz caster sugar gently for five minutes, to dissolve sugar and free the juices.

Take out one small cup of juice, then fill the basin with the fruit. Top with more slices of bread, then a plate and a heavy weight. Chill overnight. Turn out gingerly.

Pour over the reserved juice. Serve.

On the hottest days, animals pant gently in the shade, children grow fractious, insects

drone, everyone is enervated until the cool of the evening. No one eats anything, except fruit and ices. But tall glasses of cold drinks, tinkling with ice, floated with fruit, sucked through straws, are endlessly welcomed.

Iced lemon tea.

Iced coffee.

Milk shakes.

Home-made ginger beer, lemonade, elderflower or red- or black-currant cordials, topped up with soda or sparkling mineral waters. Summer punch.

Black- or Red-currant Cordial

Put 2 lb of fruit, stalks and all, into a pan with a pint of water. Cook gently until softened. Sieve or strain through a jelly-bag. Add $\frac{1}{2}$ lb of sugar to 1 pint of juice. Heat until dissolved thoroughly. Bottle when cold.

Sorbets and ices are beautiful to look at, served in tall glasses and eaten with long spoons, or in small scooped sundae dishes, or in little white china bowls. Decorated with bright bits of fruit nestling in the ice, or with a few flowers, rose petals, tiny violets, frozen into the surface.

They refresh and cleanse the mouth between savoury and sweet courses, add a zest and sparkle to the end of the meal, may be eaten alone in the middle of a hot afternoon.

No complicated equipment is necessary, only the ice-making compartment of an ordinary refrigerator, some plastic bowls or foil trays, a fork and a hand-whisk.

Water-ices can be made with any fresh berry fruit juice or puree, with lemon or grapefruit, melon, mango or mint.

Raspberry or Strawberry Ice Cream
1 lb fruit, sieved through a nylon sieve. Stir in 8 oz caster sugar until dissolved. Beat $\frac{1}{2}$ pint whipping cream until firm but not stiff. Add fruit puree and $\frac{1}{2}$ pint single cream. Pour into ice-trays or foil dishes. Freeze until firm.

Thick slabs of a good, well-kept fruit cake, or gingerbread, dark and moist, or date and walnut loaf.

Dorset Apple Cake
4 oz butter or margarine
4 oz wholemeal, 4 oz plain white flour
1½ teaspoons baking powder
8 oz chopped cooking apple
4 oz raw demerara sugar
1 egg
Pinch salt

Rub fat into flour and salt, stir in baking powder. Mix apples with sugar and stir into flour mixture. Add beaten egg and stir to form a dough.

Bake in a moderate oven for fifty-sixty minutes.

Can be spread with butter.

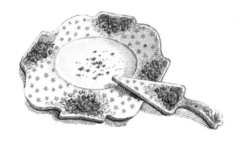

Autumn

A UTUMN cooking is for storing, squirrelling and hoarding, in larder and cupboard, attic and cellar and freezer.

In the mornings, a mist rises and wreathes in and out between the tree trunks. On the damp grass lie windfall apples and pears, burrowed into by late wasps. By noon, the sun is high,

and it is warm. The leaves are beginning to yellow and curl. Runner bean flowers are shrivelling at the tops of their poles. Fruits hang thickly clustered from their stems, over-ripe, ready to fall, plums and damsons, apples and pears, rowan and elderberries and dark succulent brambles.

* * * *

Jellies and Chutneys

IN THE kitchen stand the copper preserving pan and the wooden spoons, stained purple with last year's juices, and the empty glass jars.

It is preserving time, sticky days of making jams and jellies and chutneys and pickles. The kitchen is hot, and smells of burnt sugar and boiling fruits and spicy vinegar.

Jelly Made of Any Fruit

6 lb of fruit to 3 pints of water. Simmer until soft. Strain overnight through a jelly bag.

Allow 1 lb of sugar to 1 pint of juice. Dissolve over a gentle heat, then bring to a rolling boil, and sustain until setting point is reached. (A blob of the jelly will wrinkle when cooled on a saucer.)

Cool slightly. Pot. Label.

Make jellies of:
Bramble
Crab apple
Quince
Damson
Alone or with apple, make jellies of:
Elderberry
Rowan berry
Cranberry
Medlar

Herb jellies are excellent with cold meats, especially game.

A basic apple jelly is flavoured by suspending a bunch of fresh herbs, basil, tarragon, mint, thyme or marjoram, in the pan with the juice and sugar while it boils. This is extracted before potting.

John's Granny's Chutney

The original recipe called for thirty chillies, but possibly these were dried, and less powerful. Even using a dozen fresh chillies, the recipe is for a chutney hot enough to make one gasp and stretch one's eyes.

2 lb onions
2 lb cooking apples
2 lb tomatoes
1 cauliflower
1 small marrow
1 cucumber
2 lb demerara sugar
2 tablespoons dry mustard
1 dozen cloves
1 dozen chillies
$\frac{1}{2}$ teaspoon black pepper
$\frac{1}{2}$ teaspoon turmeric
2 tablespoons cornflour
$\frac{1}{2}$ gallon best malt vinegar

Cut up vegetables small and sweat overnight.

Mix with vinegar, sugar and spices except the turmeric. Boil for thirty minutes.

Mix mustard, cornflour and turmeric with a little cold vinegar to a paste. Add to vegetable mixture. Boil for a further thirty minutes.

Cool. Pot.

Damson Cheese

A damson cheese is a fine, old-fashioned dessert, sliced thickly and eaten cold, with cream, or with bread, or to accompany a Stilton or truckle Cheddar cheese and a glass of old port.

Wash fruit. Put in pan with water barely to cover. Simmer until soft. Rub through a sieve.

Allow 1 lb sugar to 1 lb pulp. Boil gently for one hour until very thick, taking great care not to let it stick to the pan. Test for setting.

Pot in jars or moulds. Keep for at least six months.

"The damson cheeses were sometimes poured out onto deep old dinner plates and after some days in a dry store cupboard were turned out and stacked one atop the other with spice and bay leaves between, and the whole pile covered over from dust and kept in the warm dry cupboard till shrunk and crusty with candied sugar. Such old damson cheese was a foot high, a foot across and quite hard."
Dorothy Hartley: *Food in England*

The rows of filled jars stand in the store cupboard like jewels in a treasure hoard.

Apples

"AT THE top of the house the apples are laid in rows. . . ." In the loft or the attic or the little bedroom under the eaves, they lie, carefully separated from one another, on trays and in shallow wooden crates, scenting the air.

Allington pippin
Ribston pippin
St Edmund's pippin
King of the Pippins
Blenheim Orange
James Grieve
Lady Sudeley
Lane's Prince Albert
Orleans Reinette

"There's pippins and cheese to come. . . ."
The Merry Wives of Windsor

★　　★　　★　　★

In the garden shed the marrows are slung from the beam in nets made of old nylon stockings. Onions are dried out and plaited onto straw ropes. Carrots and potatoes are layered in dark sacks.

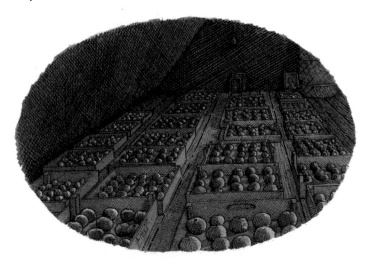

Quince

"THE STOMACH's comforter, the pleasing
quince. . ."

Sir Thomas Browne

Only a few quinces may be had, in which
case there will not be enough to make into a
jelly, except to flavour one of apple.

But they are delicious poached in sugar
syrup, left until cold, sliced and eaten with
cold meats. Or else chopped up raw and added
to a plain apple dish.

They should be picked when golden yellow and beginning to wrinkle, rubbed and
wiped carefully, then left on ledges about the
house, to fill the air with their sweet, strange,
evocative scent.

In the autumn kitchen, first preparations
are made for Christmas food. It is time to
make the Christmas cake, and a bottle of
damson and sloe gin.

Damson and Sloe Gin

1 lb damsons or sloes, pricked all over with a pin — a tedious task.

Place in a large bottle or sealable jar, with 2 spoonsful of split, blanched almonds and 4 oz caster sugar. Pour in 1 litre of gin. Seal. Shake very well to dissolve the sugar.

Leave in a cool dark cupboard for at least three months, shaking the bottle vigorously every week.

Strain and re-bottle when required.

Few things are more cheering, reviving or warming at the end of a cold winter's day than a small tot of this aromatic, ruddy liquid.

A November Dinner

Celery soup

Roast pheasant

Red cabbage and apple hot-pot

Jacket potatoes

Rowan jelly

Apple and quince tart with cream

Damson sorbet

English cheeses

A good, full Burgundy

Pumpkins

ALL THROUGH the summer, the pumpkins have been growing to magical proportions, like great orange harvest moons. In October, it is time to cut them and bear them triumphantly in, for the ceremony of weighing, and then the fun of hollowing out into grotesque heads for Hallowe'en lanterns.

The pumpkin flesh makes a good soup, with pureed spinach and some tomatoes. It can be made into the traditional American Thanksgiving Pumpkin Pie; or simply served as a vegetable, baked in chunks in the oven, dotted generously with butter and well seasoned with salt and black pepper. The giant marrows of September are equally good served in this way.

Mushrooms

ON MISTY moisty September mornings, field mushrooms may be found, nestling in the damp grass. No elaborate recipes for these, but fry them with bacon as soon as possible after picking. The smell from the pan will coax any sluggard out of bed.

Most beautiful of all, and instantly recognisable, are the scalloped, trumpet-like chanterelle or girolle mushrooms, apricot-coloured and apricot-scented, with fan vaulting below the cap, as in some ancient cathedral. They are subtle and special, best cooked in butter, with some garlic and a spoonful of thick cream, and served on hot buttered toast.

Bread

BREAD MAKING goes on all the year round, but it seems particularly significant at harvest-time, when sheaves of wheat and a bag of grain are brought to the Church altar and laid beside the freshly-baked, honey-brown harvest loaf.

A bread-making day fills the house with warm yeasty smells, and fills the freezer for weaks ahead with brown loaves and white, plaited and twisted, with baps and cobs and rolls, sprinkled with nuts and seeds, brushed with milk and honey, wonderfully risen. Everyone comes in for tea and eats new, warm crusts with butter and home-made jam.

Trestle tables in a hundred parish halls groan with produce at the autumn bazaar.

Iced cakes and fruit cakes, flapjacks and gingernuts, little trays of cherry buns and melting moments, plate pies neatly wrapped in cellophane.

Sweets

HOME-MADE sweets in doily-lined boxes, fudge and marzipan brilliantly coloured with cochineal, icing sugar fondants and peppermint creams made by children, black treacle toffee roughly broken, cocoa-dusted truffles and coconut kisses.

Rum truffles

Break 3 oz best plain chocolate into a basin. Melt gently over a pan of hot water. Remove from heat. Mix into a thick paste with 1 egg yolk, ½ oz butter and 1 teaspoonful of double cream. Form into small balls and dust in cocoa powder or roll in chocolate vermicelli strands. Makes one dozen.

In November, the autumn weather turns raw. The trees are bare, leaves lie in sodden piles rotting on the ground. Lights go on early.

There is Hallowe'en, and after that, Guy Fawkes Night, and both are good for parties with:

Sausages and chutney

Jacket potatoes and butter

Toffee apples and ginger parkin

Mugs of cocoa

After that, close the kitchen door to keep the winter out.

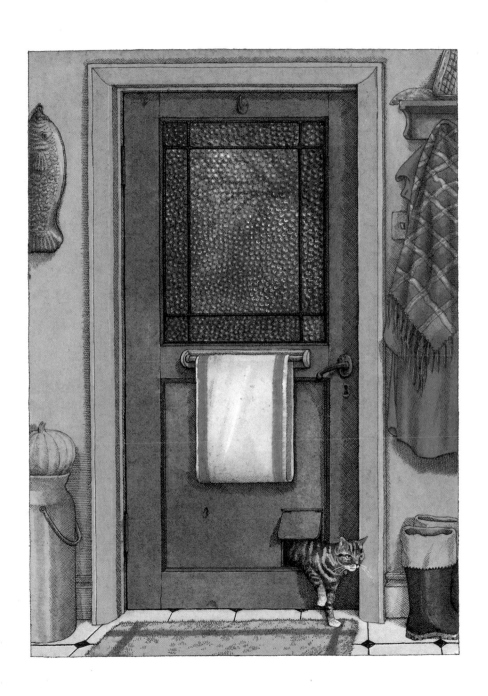